now you're cookin'
VEGETARIAN

Colophon

© 2006 Rebo International b.v., Lisse, The Netherlands

www.rebo-publishers.com – info@rebo-publishers.com

Original recipes and photographs: © R&R Publishing Pty. Ltd.

Design, layout and typesetting: AdAm Studio, Prague, The Czech Republic

Cover design: Minkowsky Graphics, Enkhuizen, The Netherlands

Proofreading: Eva Munk, Emily Sands, Sarah Dunham

Text of foreword and back cover: Emily Sands

ISBN 13: 978-90-366-1959-2

ISBN 10: 90-366-1959-9

now you're cookin'

VEGETARIAN

THIS BOOK JUST MAKES YOU WANNA COOK -

REBO
PUBLISHERS

Foreword

Societies today are fighting with obesity, the omnipresent and nutritionally deficient fast-food industry and unsanitary meatpacking plants. So it's no wonder that many people are turning to vegetarian cooking with a sigh of relief. However, tired prejudices against vegetarian cooking, fearing a lack of variety and quality – heaps of dry grains resembling birdseed against a sad backdrop of limp, overdone broccoli – are still widespread. *Creative Cooking's Vegetarian* cookbook sets out to disprove this myth and to inspire the chef. As this cookbook demonstrates, a good vegetarian diet is anything but bland. Start out with a Crunchy Snow Peas Salad and some tasty Falafel... or perhaps grilled Eggplant Kebabs. Put some Spicy Naan Bread on the side!

Contents

Method

Blanch snow peas, refresh under cold running water and drain.

Line a salad bowl with lettuce. Arrange snow peas, bean sprouts and tomato slices over lettuce.

To make dressing, place vegetable oil, sesame oil, soy, vinegar, ginger and pepper in a screw-top jar. Shake well to combine and pour over salad.

Note: Choose a variety of bean sprouts to give added flavour and texture to the salad. You might like to use alfalfa, mung bean sprouts or snow pea sprouts.

Crunchy Snow Pea Salad

Ingredients	Dressing
6½ ounces prepared	3 tablespoons vegetable oil
snow peas (mangetout)	½ teaspoon sesame oil
1 romaine lettuce	1 tablespoon soy sauce
6½ ounces mixed bean sprouts	1 tablespoon cider vinegar
1 tomato peeled, seeded and	1 teaspoon grated fresh ginger
cut in slices	freshly ground black pepper

Method

Place eggplant on a baking tray and bake for 30 minutes or until very soft. Set aside to cool, then remove skins.

Place eggplant flesh, chickpeas, yoghurt, lemon juice, garlic, mint and black pepper in a food processor or blender and process until smooth. Place dip in a serving dish and serve with warm flatbread.

Ingredients

2 eggplant

6½ ounces canned chickpeas,

drained and rinsed

1 cup low-fat

natural white yoghurt

¼ cup lemon juice

1 clove garlic, crushed

1 tablespoon chopped fresh mint

freshly ground black pepper

Chickpea and **Eggplant** Dip

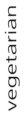

Method

Preheat the oven to 400°F. Lightly grease an 8 x 4 in loaf tin and line with baking paper.

Sift the flour and baking powder into a large mixing bowl and add the salt, rosemary and thyme.

Combine the water, yeast and sugar in a jug. Leave for 5 minutes or until the mixture is frothy.

Make a well in the flour, add the yeast mixture and oil then mix together to form a soft dough. Knead the dough on a floured surface for 5–8 minutes or until smooth. Place dough in a bowl, cover and leave in a warm place for 30–40 minutes or until doubled in size.

Punch the dough down, add the feta and knead for 2–3 mins. Place in the prepared tin, sprinkle with extra rosemary and thyme leaves, leave for 10 minutes to rise again and bake for 35–40 minutes or until golden.

Cut bread into slices and toast. Serve with ricotta and mushrooms.

To make ricotta and mushrooms, spray the mushrooms with olive oil and cook on a charcoal grill for 3 minutes on each side or until just cooked. Place a slice of ricotta on the bread, top with a mushroom, sprinkle with oregano and chili and drizzle with extra virgin olive oil.

Feta and **Herb** Bread

Ingredients

3⅓ cups all purpose flour

3 teaspoon baking powder

2 teaspoons salt

2 teaspoons rosemary leaves, dried

2 teaspoons thyme leaves, dried

1¼ cups warm water

2 x ⅓ ounce packets dried yeast

2 teaspoons sugar

1 tablespoon extra virgin olive oil

8 ounces feta cheese, crumbled

4 mushrooms (about 2 oz each)

olive oil spray

7 oz ricotta, sliced

2 teaspoons freshly chopped oregano

1 red chili, seeded and finely chopped

2 tablespoons extra virgin olive oil

Method

Melt butter in a large saucepan, add asparagus stalks, broccoli, spring onions, broad beans and 6 ounces of peas and cook, stirring, for 5 minutes.

Stir in stock and bring to a boil. Reduce heat and simmer for 15 minutes or until vegetables are tender. Using a slotted spoon, transfer vegetables to a food processor or blender and process until smooth.

Return vegetable purée to stock mixture. Add reserved asparagus tips, green beans and remaining peas and bring to a boil. Reduce heat and simmer for 5 minutes or until vegetables are tender. Season to taste with black pepper.

Note: Most soups freeze well. When freezing any liquid leave a 2 inch space between the soup and lid of the container, as liquids expand during freezing.

Ingredients

2 ounces butter

8 ounces asparagus, stalks chopped, tips reserved

8 ounces broccoli,

broken into florets

6 spring onions, chopped

8 ounces fresh or frozen broad beans

8 ounces fresh or frozen peas

4 cups vegetable stock

8 ounces green beans, cut into

1in pieces

freshly ground black pepper

Green Minestrone Soup

vegetarian

Method

Whisk together the olive oil, lemon juice, Dijon mustard, oregano and parsley in small bowl.

Brush the asparagus, haloumi and red onion with 2 tablespoons of the mixture.

Heat a barbecue plate or grill. Cook the red onion and asparagus for 2–3 minutes and the cheese for 1 minute.

Place the spinach leaves, avocado and pine nuts in a serving bowl. Add the asparagus, cheese, red onion and the remainder of the dressing. Toss to combine and serve with crusty bread.

Grilled Asparagus
and **Haloumi** Salad

Ingredients

⅓ cup olive oil

¼ cup lemon juice

2 teaspoons Dijon mustard

1 teaspoon oregano leaves, dried

1 teaspoon parsley flakes, dried

1 bunch asparagus, trimmed

8 ounces packet haloumi cheese, sliced

1 red onion, cut into wedges

3 ounces baby spinach leaves, washed and trimmed

1 avocado, sliced

¼ cup pinenuts, toasted

Method

Place soy sauce, oil, ginger, lemon juice and wine in a small bowl. Add tofu and toss to coat. Cover and set aside to marinate for 10-15 minutes.

Place lettuce, tomatoes, snow pea sprouts or watercress and carrots in a bowl. Drain tofu and reserve marinade. Add tofu to salad, toss to combine and sprinkle with sesame seeds. Just prior to serving, drizzle with reserved marinade.

Note: An easy summer meal, this salad requires only wholegrain or rye bread to make it a complete meal.

Marinated Tofu Salad

Ingredients

4 tablespoons soy sauce

2 teaspoons vegetable oil

½ teaspoon finely chopped fresh ginger

1 tablespoon lemon juice

2 teaspoons dry white wine

1 pound tofu, cut into cubes

1 head of lettuce, leaves separated

2 tomatoes, cut into wedges

2 ounces snow pea sprouts

or watercress

2 carrots, sliced

1 tablespoon sesame seeds, toasted

Method

Place avocado and lime or lemon juice in a small bowl and toss to coat.

Arrange lettuce leaves, tomatoes, green pepper, beans and avocado mixture attractively on two lunch plates. Sprinkle with coriander and season to taste with black pepper. Cover and refrigerate until required.

Note: Tossing the avocado in lime or lemon juice helps prevent it from discolouring.

Ingredients

1 avocado, pitted, peeled and chopped

1 tablespoon lime or lemon juice

lettuce leaves of your choice

2 tomatoes, cut into wedges

1 green pepper, chopped

10 ounces canned red kidney beans, drained

2 teaspoons chopped fresh coriander

freshly ground black pepper

Mexican Salad

vegetarian

Method

Place mushrooms, tomato, carrots, onion, celery, parsley, barley and water in a large saucepan and bring to a boil. Reduce heat, cover and simmer for 1 hour or until barley is tender. Season to taste with black pepper.

Ingredients

16 ounces button mushrooms, sliced

1 tomato, chopped

2 carrots, chopped

1 onion, chopped

2 stalks celery, chopped

2 tablespoons chopped fresh parsley

½ cup barley

6 cups water

freshly ground black pepper

Mushroom & Barley Soup

vegetarian

Method

Cut each naan bread into four pieces. Melt butter in a frying pan and add curry powder and sesame seeds. Cook for 1 minute. Brush mixture over the top of the bread pieces. Grill until lightly golden. Turn and grill until golden on the other side. Serve warm.

Spicy Naan Bread

Ingredients

4 naan bread

2 ounces butter

1 teaspoon mild curry powder

2 tablespoons sesame seeds

Serves **4**

Method

Arrange lettuce leaves, nashi pears, peaches, macadamia or brazil nuts and sesame seeds on a large serving platter.

To make dressing, place sesame and vegetable oils, chilli sauce and lemon juice in a screwtop jar and shake well to combine. Spoon dressing over salad and toss to combine. Cover and chill salad until required.

Note: Native to Australia, the macadamia nut has a very hard shell and a delicious, rich, buttery flavor. In most recipes that call for macadamia nuts, brazil nuts can be used instead. The nashi pear is also known as the Chinese pear and is originally from northern Asia.

If nashis are unavailable, pears or apples are a delicious alternative for this salad.

Ingredients

9½ ounces assorted lettuce leaves

2 nashi pears, cored and sliced

2 peaches, sliced

4 ounces macadamia or brazil nuts

2 tablespoons sesame seeds, toasted

Chilli-sesame dressing

2 teaspoons sesame oil

1 tablespoon vegetable oil

1 tablespoon sweet chilli sauce

2 tablespoons lemon juice

Nashi & Nut Salad

Method

Place mushrooms in a bowl. To make marinade, combine oil, lemon juice, vinegar, garlic and chilli powder in a screwtop jar. Shake well and pour over mushrooms. Toss and leave to marinate for 2-3 hours, tossing from time to time.

Gently fold in chives, parsley and pepper and serve.

Note: An all-time favorite, this mushroom salad is easy to make and delicious served as part of a salad buffet.

Raw Mushroom Salad

Ingredients	Marinade
1 pound button mushrooms, thinly sliced	½ cup olive oil
1 tablespoon finely chopped	3 tablespoons lemon juice
fresh chives	1 tablespoon white wine vinegar
1 tablespoon finely chopped fresh parsley	1 clove garlic, crushed
½ red pepper, diced	¼ teaspoon chilli powder

Method

Wash tomatoes. Cut a cross in the stem end and place in an ovenproof dish. Peel onions, cut into quarters and place around tomatoes. Peel and add garlic. Cut peppers in half, seed and add to dish. Bake at 400°F for 15 minutes. Remove from oven. Peel off tomato skins and discard. Place tomatoes, onion, garlic, peppers, chilli and basil leaves in a food processor or blender and process until pureed. Place in a saucepan with stock. Bring to a boil and simmer for 5 minutes. Serve with Bread Sticks and garnished with fresh basil.

Bread Sticks: Cut bread into eighths lengthwise. Melt margarine and brush sparingly over bread sticks. Bake at 375°F for 10 minutes or until dry and golden.

Roasted Tomato and **Pepper Soup** with Bread Sticks

Ingredients

4 pounds tomatoes

2 onions

1 clove garlic

2 red peppers

1 teaspoon prepared minced chilli

6 basil leaves or 1 teaspoon dried basil

2 cups vegetable stock

1 tablespoon torn basil leaves

BREAD STICKS

½ loaf French bread

2 tablespoons light margarine or light butter.

Method

Place tomatoes and garlic on a baking tray, sprinkle with black pepper to taste and oil and bake for 30 minutes or until tomatoes are soft and golden. Set aside to cool completely.

Arrange lettuce leaves, feta cheese, pepper, tomatoes and garlic attractively on serving plates.

To make dressing, combine vinegar, tomato purée, Tabasco and black pepper to taste in a screwtop jar and shake well. Drizzle dressing over salad and serve immediately.

Note: The sweet, rich flavor of roasted tomatoes is a perfect companion to the creamy, piquant feta cheese in this salad.

Salad of Roasted Tomatoes

Ingredients

6 plum (egg or Italian) tomatoes, halved

8 cloves garlic, peeled

freshly ground black pepper

2 tablespoons olive oil

10 ounces assorted lettuce leaves

6 ounces feta cheese, crumbled

1 yellow or red pepper, sliced

Tangy dressing

3 tablespoons balsamic or red wine vinegar

3 tablespoons tomato purée

3 drops Tabasco sauce

Method

Trim and remove strings from snow peas if necessary. Blanch snow peas and broad beans in boiling water for 2 minutes. Drain and refresh under cold water. Shell broad beans, discarding shell. Toss snow peas and broad beans. Slice peppers and add to vegetable mixture with Dressing. Mix together in a shallow bowl.

DRESSING

Crush, peel and finely chop garlic. Shake garlic, soy sauce, lime juice, fish sauce, sugar, coriander and mint together in a jar.

Snow Pea, Broad Bean and **Roasted Pepper** Salad

DRESSING

1 clove garlic

2 tablespoons soy sauce

2 tablespoons lime juice

1 tablespoon fish sauce

1 tablespoon sugar

2 tablespoons finely chopped

fresh coriander

1 tablespoon finely chopped fresh mint

Ingredients

½ pound snow peas

2 cups frozen broad beans

½ cup drained roasted red peppers

Method

Peel vegetables and prepare as necessary. Cut into ½ inch strips. Mix oils together and brush on vegetables. Grill or barbecue vegetables until they are cooked and lightly golden. Serve drizzled with Oriental Dressing and garnished with chives.

ORIENTAL DRESSING

Mix soy sauce, vinegar, black bean sauce, chilli and ginger together until combined.

Grilled Vegetables Oriental Style

Ingredients

2 medium carrots

2 parsnips

10 ounces pumpkin pieces

2 potatoes

2 zucchini

1 tablespoon oil

1 teaspoon sesame oil

fresh chives to garnish

ORIENTAL DRESSING

2 tablespoons dark soy sauce

1 tablespoon white vinegar

2 tablespoons black bean sauce

½ teaspoon prepared minced chilli

1 teaspoon grated root ginger

Method

Cut pumpkin into ½ inch chunks. Peel potatoes and cut into eight large, even-sized pieces. Cook pumpkin and potatoes with tomatoes in juice and stock. Chop apricots. Add cinnamon, ginger, cayenne pepper, lemon juice and honey. Cover and simmer for 25–30 minutes. Combine with pumpkin and potatoes and serve on a platter.

Ingredients

1 pound peeled and seeded pumpkin	¼ teaspoon ground cinnamon
4 medium potatoes	¼ teaspoon ground ginger
14 ounce can tomatoes in juice	¼ teaspoon cayenne pepper
1 cup vegetable stock	¼ cup lemon juice
6 dried apricots	1 tablespoon honey

Moroccan Potatoes and Pumpkin

37

Method

Preheat the oven to 400°F. Lightly grease a 8 x 10 inch baking dish or large oval dish.

Heat the butter in a frying pan. Add the leeks and cook for 3–4 mins or until soft.

Layer half the potatoes and sweet potatoes in the baking dish. Top with the leeks and layer with the remaining potatoes and sweet potatoes.

Combine the cream, pizza seasoning and chicken stock in a large jug. Pour over the potatoes. Sprinkle with Parmesan cheese, nutmeg and pepper. Bake in the oven for 1–11/2 hours or until the potatoes are tender. Cover with foil if the top starts to brown too much.

Potato and **Sweet Potato**
Creamy Bake

Ingredients

2 tablespoons butter

2 leeks, trimmed, halved and sliced

2 pounds potatoes, peeled and thinly sliced

1¼ pounds sweet potatoes, peeled
and thinly sliced

2 cups light cream

2 teaspoons pizza seasoning

½ cup chicken stock

2½ tablespoons grated Parmesan cheese

¼ teaspoon nutmeg, ground

black pepper, freshly ground

Method

Wash potatoes and cut into wedges. Pour oil into a roasting dish. Add potatoes and toss to coat. Sprinkle seasoning over them. Bake at 400°F for 30 minutes or until tender and golden, turning frequently during cooking. Serve hot with spiked mayo.

SPIKED MAYO

Mix mayonnaise, lemon pepper seasoning and cayenne pepper.

Potato Wedges With Spiked Mayo

Ingredients

6 large potatoes

3 tablespoons oil

2 teaspoons spicy Mexican seasoning

SPIKED MAYO

½ cup mayonnaise

1 teaspoon lemon pepper seasoning

a pinch cayenne pepper

Method

Peel potatoes and cut into wedges. Cook in boiling water for 10 minutes or until soft. Drain well. Seed chillies and finely slice. Heat oil in a frying pan and cook mustard seeds in it for 3–4 minutes or until they stop popping. Add coriander, turmeric, cumin and chillies to pan and cook for a few seconds until spices smell fragrant. Add potatoes, salt and coconut. Cook over medium heat until potatoes start to color. Sprinkle lemon juice over potatoes and continue cooking until they are crisp. Sprinkle fresh coriander or parsley over and serve.

Ingredients

6 medium potatoes

2 fresh red chillies

1/4 cup peanut oil

1 teaspoon black mustard seeds

1 teaspoon ground corianderseed

½ teaspoon ground turmeric

½ teaspoon ground cumin

½ teaspoon salt

½ cup dried coconut

¼ cup lemon juice

1 tablespoon chopped fresh coriander or parsley

Spiced Potatoes

Method

Cook noodles in boiling water in a large saucepan following packet directions. Drain, set aside and keep warm.

Heat oil in a frying pan. Add garlic and cook over medium heat, stirring, for 1 minute. Add chillies, rocket and tomatoes and cook for 2 minutes longer or until rocket wilts. Toss vegetable mixture with noodles and serve immediately.

Note: If rocket is unavailable you can use watercress instead. For a complete meal, accompany with a tossed green salad and wholemeal bread rolls.

Ingredients

1 pound buckwheat noodles

1 tablespoon olive oil

3 cloves garlic, crushed

2 fresh red chillies,
seeded and chopped

6½ ounces rocket leaves
separated and shredded

2 tomatoes, chopped

Spicy Buckwheat Noodles

45

Method

Mix yoghurt, ginger, chilli powder, coriander and boiling water together. Mix potato in until smooth. Add rice flour and mix to combine. Heat a heavy-based, ovenproof frying pan until very hot. Grease base with sesame oil. Spread potato mixture into pan and bake at 400°F for 20–25 minutes or until lightly golden.

Ingredients

½ cup unsweetened natural yoghurt

1 teaspoon prepared minced ginger

½–1 teaspoon chilli powder

3 tablespoons chopped fresh coriander

1½ cups boiling water

1½ cups instant mashed potatoes

¼ cup rice flour

1 teaspoon sesame oil

Spicy Potato Roti

Method

Peel onion and chop finely. Crush, peel and chop garlic. Heat oil in a medium saucepan and sauté onion and garlic until glassy. Add two cups of water and bring to a boil. Peel sweet potatoes and cut into even-sized pieces. Place in boiling water and onion mixture and cook for 15–20 minutes or until soft. Drain all but quarter of a cup of cooking water from sweet potatoes. Mash until smooth. Mix in chilli and coriander and beat with a fork until smooth. Serve hot as a mash or form into Sweet Potato Cakes.

SWEET POTATO CAKES

Measure quarter cupfuls of mixture and shape into balls with floured hands. Flatten balls and cook in hot oil until golden on both sides. Serve with pineapple salsa or sweet chilli sauce. Makes 12 cakes.

Sweet Potato Mash

Ingredients

1 onion

1 clove garlic

1 tablespoon oil

4 medium sweet potatoes

2 teaspoons prepared minced chilli

2 tablespoons chopped fresh coriander

Method

Prepare the vegetables, peeling, trimming and chopping as necessary. Cut into even-sized pieces. Peel onions and chop finely. Heat oil in a saucepan and sauté onion for 5 minutes. Add curry powder and sauté for 1 minute. Mix in coconut cream. Bring to a boil. Add vegetables. Cover and simmer until vegetables are tender. Mix in chilli and soy sauces. Serve garnished with sliced red chilli.

Vegetable Curry

Ingredients

1 pound mixed fresh seasonal vegetables such

as pumpkin, parsnip, broccoli, beans, etc

2 onions

1 tablespoon oil

1 tablespoon hot curry powder

10 ounce can coconut cream

1 tablespoon sweet chilli sauce

1 tablespoon soy sauce

1 fresh red chilli, to garnish

Method

Heat oil in a large frying pan, add garlic, leeks and carrots and cook, stirring, for 5 minutes or until leeks are tender. Add tomatoes, bring to a boil, then reduce heat and simmer for 10 minutes or until mixture reduces and thickens. Stir in beans and cook for 3-4 minutes longer. Season to taste with black pepper.

Transfer bean mixture to a greased ovenproof dish, top with mashed potato and sprinkle with cheese. Bake for 20 minutes or until top is golden.

Bean Cottage Pie

Ingredients

1 tablespoon vegetable oil	14 ounce canned lima or butter beans, drained
2 cloves garlic, crushed	freshly ground black pepper
2 leeks, white parts only, sliced	1½lb potatoes, cooked
2 large carrots, sliced	and mashed
14 ounce can crushed tomatoes, undrained	2 ounces grated mature cheese

Method

To make filling, heat oil in a large frying pan, add onion and cook for 5 minutes. Stir in taco seasoning and chilli powder and cook for 1 minute longer.

Add red pepper and zucchini and cook, stirring, for 3-4 minutes. Stir in beans, crushed tomatoes and tomato paste, simmer for 10 minutes or until mixture reduces and thickens.

Place taco shells on a baking tray and heat in the oven for 5 minutes. Half-fill each taco shell with filling, then top with avocado slices and serve immediately with cottage cheese, lettuce, chopped tomato and chilli sauce, if desired.

Ingredients

12 taco shells

1 avocado, sliced and brushed with

2 tablespoons lemon juice

4 ounces cottage cheese

¼ head of lettuce, shredded

1 tomato, chopped

1 tablespoon chilli sauce (optional)

Spicy bean filling:

1 tablespoon vegetable oil

1 onion, chopped

1½ ounces packet taco seasoning

Bean-filled Tacos

¼ teaspoon chilli powder

1 red pepper, chopped

1 zucchini, chopped

10 ounce canned red kidney beans, drained

14 ounce can crushed tomatoes, undrained

3 tablespoons tomato paste

Method

To make filling, melt butter in a small frypan. Add ginger, bean sprouts and chives and cook for 1 minute. Remove from pan and keep warm.

To make omelette, melt butter in a small frypan. Lightly whisk together eggs and water and season with pepper. Pour into pan and cook over medium heat. Continually draw the edge of the omelette in with a fork during cooking until no liquid remains and the omelette is lightly set.

Sprinkle the bean sprout mixture over the omelette and fold in half. Slip onto a plate and serve immediately.

Bean Sprout Omelette

Filling

1 teaspoon butter

2 tablespoons grated fresh ginger

4 tablespoons bean sprouts

4 chives, finely chopped

Omelette

1 teaspoon butter

2 eggs

2 teaspoons water

freshly ground black pepper

Method

Preheat the oven to 400°F.

Place the cauliflower and broccoli in a microwave or oven-proof dish. Add 2 tablespoons water, cover with plastic and microwave on high for 4 minutes. Drain the water from the vegetables and set aside.

Heat the butter in a saucepan. Stir in the flour. Remove from the heat and slowly add the milk, stirring continuously. Return to the heat, stir in the mustard, nutmeg, and salt and pepper to taste along with half the cheese. Stir until the mixture is smooth and thickens.

Pour the sauce over the cauliflower and broccoli, top with remaining cheese and bake in the oven for 12–15 minutes or until golden on top.

Ingredients

10 ounces cauliflower, cut into florets

10 ounces broccoli, cut into florets

Cauliflower and Broccoli Bake

Cheese Sauce

2 tablespoons butter

¼ cup all purpose flour

1⅔ cups milk

2 teaspoons mild English or Dijon mustard

¼ teaspoon nutmeg, ground

salt and freshly ground black pepper

1 cup grated white cheddar

Method

Place mushrooms in a bowl and cover with boiling water. Set aside to stand for 15-20 minutes or until mushrooms are tender. Drain, remove stalks if necessary and slice mushrooms.

Heat oil in a wok or frying pan, add garlic, ginger and onion and stir-fry over medium heat for 3 minutes or until onion is soft.

Add red pepper, carrots, broccoli and celery and stir-fry for 3 minutes longer.

Add mushrooms, sweet corn, tofu, chilli sauce, soy sauce and cashews and stir-fry for 1 minute longer. Serve immediately.

Ingredients

3½ ounces dried mushrooms

2 teaspoons sesame oil

2 cloves garlic, crushed

1 tablespoon grated fresh ginger

1 large onion, sliced

1 red pepper, cut into strips

2 carrots, sliced diagonally

8 ounces broccoli, cut into florets

3 stalks celery, sliced diagonally

11 onces canned baby sweet

Easy Vegetable Stir-fry

corn, drained

6½ ounces firm tofu, chopped

2 tablespoons sweet chilli sauce

2 tablespoons soy sauce

2 ounces cashew nuts

Method

Place garlic, oil and cumin in a small bowl and whisk to combine. Brush oil mixture over cut sides of eggplant.

Thread eggplant onto lightly oiled skewers and cook on a hot grill or under a preheated hot grill for 4 minutes each side or until tender.

To make sauce, combine yoghurt, coriander and mint. Serve sauce with hot kebabs.

Note: For a complete meal, accompany this dish with pita bread and a salad.

Ingredients

2 cloves garlic, crushed

1 tablespoon vegetable oil

2 teaspoons ground cumin

8 baby eggplants,

sliced in half, lengthwise

Eggplant Kebabs

Yoghurt sauce

¾ cup natural yoghurt

2 tablespoons chopped fresh coriander

2 tablespoons chopped fresh mint

vegetarian

63

Method

Place chickpeas in a large bowl, cover with cold water and set aside to soak overnight. Drain. Place chickpeas in large saucepan, cover with water and bring to a boil.

Boil for 10 minutes, then reduce heat and simmer for 45-60 minutes or until chickpeas are tender. Drain and set aside to cool.

Place chickpeas, garlic, onion, spring onions, coriander, parsley, cumin and turmeric in a food processor or blender and process to combine.

Heat oil in a large saucepan. Shape tablespoons of chickpea mixture into balls and deep-fry, a few at a time, for 3 minutes or until golden brown. Drain on absorbent kitchen paper.

Note: For speedier preparation, omit Step 1 and use canned chickpeas. You will need two 14 ounce cans and the chickpeas should be drained and rinsed before making the falafel.

Ingredients

14 ounces chickpeas

3 cloves garlic, crushed

1 small onion, chopped

4 spring onions, chopped

2 tablespoons chopped fresh coriander

2 tablespoons chopped fresh parsley

1 teaspoon ground cumin

½ teaspoon turmeric

vegetable oil, for deep frying

Falafels

Method

Place red kidney and black-eyed beans in a large bowl, cover with water and set aside to soak overnight. Drain. Bring a large saucepan of water to a boil, add beans and boil for 10 minutes. Reduce heat and simmer for 1 hour or until beans are tender. Drain and set aside.

Heat oil in a large saucepan over medium heat, add garlic and onion and cook, stirring, for 3 minutes or until onion is soft and golden. Add tomatoes, cumin, mustard, golden syrup and tomato paste and bring to a boil. Reduce heat and simmer for 5 minutes

Add cooked beans, carrots, zucchini, butter beans, broad beans and oregano to pan and simmer for 30 minutes or until vegetables are tender.

Note: All types of beans adapt to a huge range of seasonings. The beans in this casserole can be varied to accommodate whatever you have available.

As an alternative, try a combination of haricot and butter beans with chickpeas, and substitute your favourite spices or dried herbs for the ground cumin and oregano.

Ingredients

5 ounces dried red kidney beans

5 ounces dried black-eyed beans

1 tablespoon vegetable oil

2 cloves garlic, crushed

1 red onion, chopped

14 ounces canned peeled tomatoes, undrained and crushed

1 tablespoon ground cumin

1 tablespoon dry mustard

Hearty Bean Casserole

2 tablespoons golden syrup

1 tablespoon tomato paste

2 carrots, thickly sliced

3 zucchini, thickly sliced

14 ounces canned butter beans, rinsed and drained

3½ ounces shelled broad beans, fresh or frozen

2 tablespoons chopped fresh oregano or 1 teaspoon dried oregano

vegetarian

Method

Place lentils in a large saucepan, cover with water and bring to a boil. Reduce heat and simmer for 30 minutes or until lentils are tender. Drain and set aside.

Melt butter in a large saucepan, add onion and garlic and cook over medium heat, stirring, for 5 minutes or until onion is soft. Add carrots, tomato, oregano and water and bring to a boil. Reduce heat and simmer for 10 minutes or until carrots are tender.

Add spinach, lemon juice and lentils to pan, and simmer for 15 minutes or until mixture reduces and thickens.

Spoon lentil mixture into pita bread pockets and serve immediately.

Lentil Pockets

Ingredients

6½ ounces red lentils

½ teaspoon butter

1 onion, chopped

2 cloves garlic, crushed

3 carrots, chopped

1 tomato, chopped

1 tablespoon chopped fresh oregano or

1 teaspoon dried oregano

½ cup water

1 pound fresh spinach, stalks removed and leaves chopped

1 tablespoon lemon juice

6 large pita bread rounds, warmed and cut in half

Method

Heat oil in a large saucepan. Add garlic, chillies and onions and cook over medium heat, stirring constantly, for 5 minutes or until onions are soft and golden.

Add okra, eggplant, tomatoes, beans, tofu, wine and sugar. Bring to a boil, then reduce heat and simmer for 30 minutes. Stir in basil and black pepper to taste.

Note: Serve this tasty vegetable stew with wholemeal pasta or brown rice.

When preparing fresh okra, wash it well and handle it carefully. Rub it gently under running water to remove the fuzzy outer layer.

ingredients

2 teaspoons vegetable oil

2 cloves garlic, crushed

2 fresh red chillies, chopped

2 onions, sliced

8 ounces okra

2 eggplants, chopped

2 x 14 ounce cans peeled tomatoes, undrained and crushed

14 ounces canned red kidney beans, rinsed

8 ounces firm tofu, cut into chunks

½ cup red wine

1 tablespoon brown sugar

3 tablespoons chopped fresh basil

freshly ground black pepper

Okra & Bean Stew

vegetarian

Method

Melt butter in a large frying pan. Cook garlic one minute. Add parsnips and carrot and cook over medium heat,stirring occasionally, until almost cooked.

Season with rosemary, parsley and pepper.

Transfer to greased, shallow, ovenproof dish and pour in cream. Spinkle with breadcrumbs and cheese and dot with butter. Bake in a preheated 400°F oven for 35 minutes or until browned.

Parsnip and **Carrot** Bake

Ingredients

2 ounces butter	ground black pepper to taste
2 cloves garlic, crushed	1½ cups fresh breadcrumbs
1 pound parsnips, washed and grated	3 tablespoons Parmesan cheese, grated
10 ounces carrot, peeled and grated	1 teaspoon dried rosemary leaves
1¼ cups cream	1 teaspoon dried parsley flakes

Method

Preheat the oven to 425°F.

Combine the squash, 1 tablespoon olive oil, balsamic vinegar, salt and pepper in a non-stick baking tray. Bake in the oven for 20–25 minutes or until the squash is golden.

Meanwhile, place the vegetable bouillon in a saucepan. Bring to a boil and simmer gently.

Heat the remaining oil in a large saucepan over medium heat. Cook the onion and garlic for 2–3 minutes or until soft. Add the rice and stir until combined.

Add 1 cup of the bouillon and the rosemary leaves. Cook, stirring from time to time, until all the liquid is absorbed. Repeat this until the bouillon is gone and the rice is tender.

Stir in the squash, goat cheese, baby spinach and parsley and season to taste. Cook until heated through and the spinach has wilted.

Serve immediately with crusty bread.

Roasted Squash Risotto

Ingredients

1 lb butternut squash, peeled and cut into

¾in cm pieces

2 tablespoons olive oil

2 teaspoons balsamic vinegar

salt and freshly ground black pepper

5 cups vegetable bouillon

1 onion, finely chopped

3 cloves garlic, freshly crushed

2 cups arborio rice

1 teaspoon rosemary leaves, dried

4 ounces goat cheese, crumbled

5 ounces baby spinach leaves, washed and trimmed

¼ cup freshly chopped parsley leaves

Method

Preheat the oven to 425°F.

Place the potatoes and sweet potatoes on a non-stick baking tray. Drizzle with 11/2 table-spoons oil and season with salt and pepper. Toss to combine and bake in the oven for 10 minutes, turning from time to time. Add the zucchini and red bell pepper and bake for a further 15 minutes, turning from time to time.

Heat the remaining oil in a 9 inch, non-stick, heavy-based frying pan over medium heat. Cook the leeks and garlic for 3–4 minutes. Stir in 1 teaspoon Italian herbs. Add the vegetables and toss to combine.

Whisk together the eggs, sour cream, milk, Parmesan cheese, dried peppers and the remaining herbs in a bowl. Pour the egg mixture over the vegetables. Reduce the heat to low and cook for 12–15 minutes or until nearly cooked.

Place the frying pan under a hot grill for 4–5 minutes or until golden and cooked. Place a pot holder around the handle before removing from the grill.

Cut the frittata into wedges and serve with crusty bread and salad.

Roasted Vegetable Frittata

Ingredients

8 ounces new potatoes, cut into quarters in slices

8 ounces sweet potatoes, peeled, halved and cut into quarters

2½ tablespoons olive oil

salt and freshly ground black pepper

1 large zucchini, halved and sliced

1 red bell pepper, seeded and diced

1 leek, trimmed, halved, washed and sliced

1 clove garlic, freshly crushed

2 teaspoons Italian herbs

1 teaspoon dried bell pepper

6 eggs, lightly beaten

½ cup light sour cream

¼ cup milk

½ cup grated Parmesan cheese

Method

Preheat oven to 350°F.

Brush each sheet of pastry with oil and fold in half. Layer pastry, one folded piece on top of the other, making eight layers. Place a 7 inch flan dish upside down on layered pastry and cut around dish, making a circle 1¼ inch larger. Lift all layers of pastry into dish and roll edges.

Cook onion in a frying pan for 4-5 minutes or until opaque and soft. Place pumpkin or carrots, cheese, egg yolks, sour cream or yoghurt, chilli powder and black pepper to taste in a bowl and mix to combine.

Place egg whites in a bowl and beat until stiff peaks form. Fold egg white mixture into pumpkin mixture and spoon into pastry case. Sprinkle pumpkin mixture with parsley and bake for 30 minutes or until pastry is golden and cooked.

Note: When incorporating beaten egg whites into the mixture, first stir in 1 tablespoon of beaten egg white, then lightly fold in the remaining beaten egg white, working as quickly as possible.

Ingredients

4 sheets filo pastry

2 tablespoons vegetable oil

1 onion, chopped

8 ounces pumpkin or carrots, cooked and mashed

6 ounces grated cheese (mature Cheddar)

2 eggs, separated

2 tablespoons sour cream or natural yoghurt

a pinch chilli powder

freshly ground black pepper

1 tablespoon chopped fresh parsley

Savory Pumpkin Quiche

79

Method

To make dressing, place yoghurt, coriander, ginger, chilli sauce, garlic and black pepper to taste in a bowl and mix to combine.

To make burgers, place soy beans in a food processor or blender and process to roughly chop. Place chopped beans, breadcrumbs, onion, carrot, flour, mint, ginger and egg in a bowl and mix well to combine. Shape mixture into six burgers and roll each in sesame seeds.

Heat oil in a frying pan over medium heat, add burgers and cook for 6 minutes on each side or until heated through and golden.

Top bottom half of each roll with a lettuce leaf, a burger, a few alfalfa sprouts, tomato slices, beetroot, sunflower seeds, a spoonful of dressing and the top half of the roll. Serve immediately.

Note: Besan flour is made from chickpeas and is available from Asian and health food stores (you can substitute pea flour made from split peas, if desired). To make your own besan flour, place chickpeas on a baking tray and bake at 350°F for 15-20 minutes or until roasted. Cool, then grind using a food processor or blender to a fine flour.

Ingredients

6 multigrain rolls, split and toasted

6 lettuce leaves of your choice

1 ounce alfalfa sprouts

2 large tomatoes, sliced

1 raw beetroot, grated

4 tablespoons sunflower seeds, toasted

Minted soy burgers

14 ounces canned soy beans, rinsed and drained

1 cup wholemeal breadcrumbs, made from stale bread

1 red onion, finely chopped

1 carrot, grated

Soy Burgers

3 tablespoons chickpea flour

3 tablespoons chopped fresh mint

1 tablespoon finely grated fresh ginger

1 egg, lightly beaten

2½ ounces sesame seeds

2 tablespoons vegetable oil

Creamy dressing

1 cup natural yoghurt

1 tablespoon chopped fresh coriander

1 tablespoon grated fresh ginger

2 tablespoons sweet chilli sauce

1 clove garlic, crushed

freshly ground black pepper

vegetarian

Method

Cut ciabatta in half lengthwise. Spray with oil and grill until lightly golden. Remove from oven and arrange grilled vegetables over one half of the bread. Mix mayonnaise, yoghurt, tandoori curry powder, chives and lemon juice. Drizzle over vegetables. Top with remaining bread half. Cut into ¾ inch slices to serve.

Ingredients

1 large ciabatta

oil spray

about 4 cups mixed chargrilled vegetables such

as peppers, eggplant and zucchini

½ cup mayonnaise

½ cup unsweetened natural yoghurt

1 teaspoon tandoori curry powder

2 tablespoons chopped fresh chives

1 tablespoon lemon juice

Spicy Chargrilled
Vegetable Ciabatta

vegetarian

Method

Grill tortillas on both sides until lightly golden and keep warm. Peel onion and chop finely. Melt butter in a frying pan and sauté onion for 5 minutes until clear. Lightly beat eggs, chilli powder, paprika and milk together. Pour into frying pan with onion and cook over medium heat until egg begins to set. Drag a wooden spatula through egg mixture to allow uncooked egg to run through to the base of the pan. Spread salsa over tortillas to within ¾ inch of the edge. Pile scrambled eggs on top. Slice tomatoes. Peel, de-stone and slice avocado. Garnish eggs with tomato and avocado slices.

Spicy Mexican Scrambled Eggs

Ingredients

4 flour tortillas

1 small onion

1 tablespoon butter

6 eggs

½ teaspoon chilli powder

½ teaspoon paprika

¼ cup milk

6 ounce jar chunky salsa

2 tomatoes, to garnish

1 avocado, to garnish

Method

Preheat the oven to 350°F. Lightly grease an 8 inch square ovenproof pie dish.

Heat the butter in a small saucepan. Add the leeks and cook until soft.

Remove the hard red stem from the Swiss chard and shred the leaves. Cook in a large saucepan of boiling water for 2 minutes or until bright green and wilted. Drain and rinse under cold water. Squeeze out excess water.

Mix together the leeks, Swiss chard, feta cheese, cottage cheese, Parmesan cheese, eggs, Italian herbs, nutmeg and pepper in a large bowl.

Spoon the mixture into the prepared pie dish.

Place 2 sheets of filo pastry on a clean surface. Brush with the melted butter and repeat with the remaining pastry. Place the pastry on top of the pie. Trim to the edge of the dish and tuck in the overhanging pastry. Brush with the remaining butter, sprinkle with sesame seeds and bake for 45 minutes or until golden and cooked.

Cut into slices and serve with a green salad.

Ingredients

2 tablespoons butter

1 leek, trimmed, washed and sliced

1 large bunch Swiss chard, washed

5 ounces feta cheese, crumbled

8 ounces low-fat cottage cheese

⅓ cup grated Parmesan cheese

4 eggs, lightly beaten

1 tablespoon Italian herbs

¼ teaspoon nutmeg, ground

freshly ground black pepper

6 sheets filo pastry

1 tablespoon melted butter

1 tablespoon sesame seeds

Spinach and **Feta** Pie

Method

Peel pumpkin, seed and cut into even-sized pieces. Peel onion and chop finely. Crush, peel and finely chop garlic. Heat oil in a saucepan and sauté onion and garlic for 5 minutes. Add curry powder and chilli powder and cook for 1 minute or until spices smell fragrant. Add water and bring to a boil. Add pumpkin and cook for 15 minutes or until pumpkin is just cooked. Wash spinach and remove stems. Tear coarse leaves into pieces. Add to pumpkin mixture and cook for 2–3 minutes. Cut tomatoes in half. Remove seeds and chop flesh into small cubes. Fold into pumpkin mixture. Serve on a platter.

Spinach and **Pumpkin** Curry

Ingredients

2 pounds pumpkin

1 large onion

2 cloves garlic

2 tablespoons oil

2 teaspoons Madras curry powder

½ teaspoon chilli powder

1½ cups water

3 bunches spinach

2 tomatoes

Method

To make pancakes, boil or microwave spinach or silverbeet until wilted. Drain and squeeze out as much liquid as possible.

Place flour in a bowl and make a well in the center. Add eggs and a little of the milk and beat, working in all the flour. Beat in butter and remaining milk.

Pour 2-3 tablespoons of batter into a 8 inch nonstick frying pan and tilt pan so batter evenly covers base. Cook for 1 minute on each side or until lightly browned. Set aside and keep warm. Repeat with remaining batter.

To make filling, heat oil in a frying pan, add garlic and cook over medium heat, stirring, for 1 minute. Add spinach or silverbeet and cook for 3 minutes longer or until spinach or silverbeet wilts.

Stir in sour cream or yoghurt and black pepper to taste. Spread a spoonful of filling over each crepe. Fold crepes into quarters and serve immediately.

Note: These wholesome crepes envelop a delicious savoury filling and are best served immediately after cooking.

Ingredients

8 spinach or silverbeet leaves, shredded

1 cup flour

4 eggs, lightly beaten

⅔ cup milk

1 ounce butter, melted

Spinach Crepes

Spinach filling

2 teaspoons vegetable oil

2 cloves garlic, crushed

12 spinach or silverbeet leaves, shredded

9½ ounces sour cream or

natural yoghurt

freshly ground black pepper

Method

Drain corn. Trim zucchini and grate coarsely. Mix corn, zucchini, flour, baking powder, eggs, milk and sweet chilli sauce together until batter is smooth. Mix oils together and heat in a heavy-based frying pan. Cook quarter cupfuls of corn mixture in hot oil until golden and cooked on both sides. Cut cucumber in half and remove seeds. Cut flesh into ½ inch cubes. Mix with sweet chilli sauce and serve with corn and zucchini cakes.

Ingredients

14 ounce can whole kernel corn

2 medium zucchini

½ cup flour

1 teaspoon baking powder

2 eggs

½ cup milk

3 tablespoons sweet Thai chilli sauce

1 teaspoon sesame oil

2 tablespoons oil

½ cucumber

¼ cup sweet Thai chilli sauce

Sweet Chilli,
Corn and Zucchini Fritters

Method

Combine olive oil, black peppercorns and lemon juice and brush over eggplant slices. Cook eggplant under a preheated medium grill for 3-4 minutes on each side or until golden. Set aside.

Place breadcrumbs and Parmesan cheese in a bowl, mix to combine and set aside.

Heat a nonstick frying pan, add onion, garlic and reserved tomato juice and cook over medium heat, stirring, for 5 minutes or until onion is soft. Add tomatoes, tomato purée, wine, oregano, basil and cayenne pepper and cook for 5 minutes longer.

Spread one-third of the tomato mixture over base of a 6 by10 inch ovenproof dish. Top with 3 lasagne sheets, half the breadcrumb mixture and cover with a layer of eggplant. Top with half the ricotta cheese. Repeat layers, ending with a layer of tomato mixture. Sprinkle with mozzarella cheese and bake for 45 minutes.

Note: As an accompaniment to this hearty lasagne, try a light salad or steamed mixed vegetables.

Vegetable Lasagne

Ingredients

1 tablespoon olive oil

½ teaspoon crushed black peppercorns

3 tablespoons lemon juice

1 large eggplant (aubergine), halved lengthwise and cut into

¼ inch slices

½ cup wholemeal breadcrumbs, made from stale bread

3 tablespoons grated Parmesan cheese

1 large onion, chopped

2 cloves garlic, crushed

14 ounce canned tomatoes, drained, chopped and 1 tablespoon juice reserved

¾ cup tomato purée

2 tablespoons white wine

1 teaspoon dried oregano

1 teaspoon dried basil

pinch cayenne pepper

6 sheets instant (no precooking required) wholemeal lasagne

6 ounces ricotta cheese

3 tablespoons grated mozzarella cheese